God
is Still Calling

God
is Still Calling

How to Listen to God's Voice in a World Full of Noise

JAY HANSON

invite
PRESS
Plano, Texas

Table of Contents

Acknowledgements

To all who invest the time to read this, may God use it to help you learn to hear and recognize His voice.

To my family,

Rev. Dave and Kay Hanson (Mom & Dad) thank you for continuing to help me learn to listen to God and for modeling a healthy marriage for 65 years.

Kim, thank you for being my wife and partner in life. You live out love better than anyone I know. Cole & Bailey, Summer & Chris, as you continue on your spiritual journeys, I hope you will always remember God loves you and Daddy does too. I pray that you learn to listen to God and do whatever He says.

Judge Jeff Hanson, you are the best brother a man could hope to have, and I am deeply thankful for how you have listened to God all your life. Thank you for leading me well.

To The Chapel Family,

It has been a joy to serve with you for the past 20 years. God has and is doing some great things here and I am glad I have gotten to be on the journey with you. It is an honor to be your pastor and friend.

To those who hear God,

God is still calling!!!! I believe He is calling some of you who will use this devotional to go to seminary to learn more about hearing and responding to God. If that is you, Kim and I want to help you. We have decided to dedicate the proceeds we get from any sales of this book to provide scholarships to Asbury Theological Seminary and Wesleyan Biblical Seminary. Simply notify the registrar at the school you read *God is Still Calling* and would like some financial support for your tuition and they will help you, depending on available funds.

Introduction

If the Christian does not know when God is speaking, they
are in trouble at the heart of their Christian life.
– Henry Blackaby in *Experiencing God*

There is nothing more essential than the ability to recognize, hear, and understand the voice of God. It is the foundation of a faithful life. I am still learning how to listen to God, but I am becoming increasingly aware of the need for it and the normal absence of it.

Words fascinate me. For instance, the word "hear" contains the word "ear." Even more interesting is how the word "heart" contains the word "hear." "Hear" plus "t" equals "heart," perhaps suggesting the heart means to hear the cross. The heart of the matter for me and the point of this book is to help all of us become more receptive and responsive to the leadings of God. This requires the belief that God is speaking to us and that we take the time to pay attention to what He is saying.

There is nothing unusual or special about my story, but my story does illustrate how God uses ordinary people and normal things to do amazing miracles. My hope is hearing my story will not simply help you see what is possible but also help you begin to understand that it is normal and to be expected.

God is constantly speaking to all of us. Leading us. Guiding us. Letting us know He loves us and is with us. When our activity is not directed by Him, it will not be fruitful or fulfilling. We will be busy but not effective and will eventually burn out. Listening to God not only brings power to our actions, but it also keeps us connected relationally with God, giving our lives meaning and purpose. Sometimes we want a manual that tells us what to do, but God gave us an Emmanuel who walks with us and who works through us.

Jesus said, "I am the vine; you are the branches. If you remain in me and I in you, you will bear much fruit; apart from me you can do nothing" (John 15:5).

We tend to want to direct our attention and put our energy in the "bear much fruit" part but notice what comes before the comma. "*If* you remain in me," *then* you will automatically bear much fruit. Learning to listen to God is all about remaining, abiding, staying connected to, and walking with God. Without learning to listen to God we can do nothing because there is nothing more essential than the ability to recognize, hear, and understand the voice of God. It is how we remain in Him.

How to Use This Guidebook

This devotional on learning to listen to God is designed to be a short, easy to use guidebook to help you begin to incorporate spiritual listening into your daily life of following Christ. My aim is to help you cultivate your capacity to notice, discern, and respond to God's voice in your life.

Each day's entry is divided into five key parts:

- A key **theme** or concept of the day
- A **scripture** reading that emphasizes how the Spirit speaks to us
- A personal **reflection** from my journey of learning to listen to the Holy Spirit
- A **question** to assist you in cultivating your own honest and authentic reflection
- A **prayer** to keep you focused on the presence of the Holy Spirit throughout the day.

At the end of each week, there is a Practical Application. These entries also have a key concept, a question, and a prayer, but instead of a scripture and personal reflection, they have Action Steps to help you practically apply the week's lessons.

The last day of the week is a Recap & Reflect entry. These days have a Recap instead of a personal reflection. These days also have a key concept, reflection question, and prayer.

Once you've completed this guidebook, my hope is that you will find that learning to listen has become a practical and accessible part of your regular walk with Jesus.

Note this guidebook is also designed for group use. Use the questions to connect with others who are navigating their own 28-day spiritual journey, so that you have companions with whom you can read, learn, share, discuss, and pray.

If you are a pastor or church leader, I invite you to consider using this guidebook at your church as the basis of a congregation-wide, 28-day journey of learning to listen.

Finally, be confident that as you listen, God's voice will fill you and guide you beyond what you could ever ask, think, or imagine (Ephesians 3:20).

Week 1: God Woos.
Exodus 3:1–3

Theme:

God woos us to enter the silence and learn to listen to the inner conversation with God that is already occurring.

Introduction:

Listening to God begins with quieting the noise around us and within us. We live in a world full of distractions—busy schedules, constant notifications, and the relentless pressure to do more. It's easy to rush through life without pausing to notice the signs of God's presence.

As we learn to enter the silence, we discover God isn't silent. He's always speaking, waiting for us to pay attention. Just as Moses encountered God in the burning bush, we can find Him in the ordinary moments of our lives—if we learn to slow down and listen.

This week, we'll explore what it means to enter the silence. We'll reflect on stories like Moses' desert encounter and examine how God uses the everyday to reveal the extraordinary. Together, we'll take the first steps toward cultivating a spirit of listening.

Day 1: Show Up to Work

Key Concept:

We can literally encounter God anywhere if we learn to pay attention.

Scripture:

Now Moses was tending the flock of Jethro his father-in-law, the priest of Midian, and he led the flock to the far side of the wilderness and came to Horeb, the mountain of God.

— Exodus 3:1

Reflection:

The burning bush story of Moses' calling is one of the best-known stories of the Bible, and this historic encounter sets in motion a major facet of God's plan to liberate a people who would become His people and from whom the Messiah would come and provide a way for all people to become His people. On this day, through this encounter, world history pivots! Looking back, it is easy to see how big a deal this day was, but for Moses it started out as just another Monday.

Moses wasn't going on the Walk to Emmaus or any special spiritual retreat. He was just going to work, just like he had every day for the past 40 years. He woke up early and packed his lunch and headed to the office, which for him happened to be on "the far side of the wilderness" this week.

It was a Tuesday for me. I woke up at 3:30am and headed out. I wasn't headed to work; I was taking the weekly four hour drive to Orlando, Florida where I was taking classes at Asbury Seminary. Typically, I would arrive in time for my 8:00am class. I would skip lunch and the chapel service to take a nap, then do an afternoon class followed by a five hour drive through rush hour traffic back to St. Simons Island, Georgia where I lived and worked. This was my routine, and I had been doing it for years, but this Tuesday turned out to be very different.

Maxie Dunham was leading the chapel service this Tuesday. At the time, I didn't know Maxie, but I had read some of his writings and was familiar with who he was, so I thought I would skip my normal nap and sit it on the service. Honestly, I don't remember the text he taught or much of what he said, but I will never forget an exercise he had us do. He paired us up with another person in the room. As he was doing so, I remember quickly scanning the room and thinking there is only one person in here that I absolutely do not want to be paired with. Yep, you guessed it; I was paired with them.

The exercise was pretty straightforward and simple. We were to sit facing each other and simply say "The Christ in me greets the Christ in you." There may have been more that was supposed to follow, but I don't remember anything past that. As my partner said the words to me, I was thinking to myself, "I am pretty sure Christ is not in you," but I figured I would play along. So, I listened and politely smiled, until it was my turn to speak. When they had finished, I began. "The Christ in me greets the Christ in you," I said, and when I did, something happened.

Something broke loose in me. I was in the presence of God again. I had not even realized how far from God I had drifted. I hadn't noticed I had lost my awareness of the nearness of God, but in that moment, I knew I was with God again, and I knew I didn't ever want to leave.

Today, as we begin this journey together for the next 27 days, let me say "The Christ in me greets the Christ in you." As you prepare to simply show up at work today like you do every day, I pray you will notice how close God is to you today and that each day on this journey together you will become increasingly aware of the nearness of God.

Reflection Question:

If God captured your full attention today, what do you think He might want to say to you?

Prayer:

Lord, speak for your servant is listening. As I enter this day, may I become increasingly aware of your nearness and may my ear be tuned to hear your voice. Help me to see where you are moving and give me the courage to join you. Amen.

Day 2: Every Day in Every Way

Key Concept:

See God in the ordinary and discover He is constantly communicating with those who will listen.

Scripture:

Now Moses was tending the flock of Jethro his father-in-law, the priest of Midian, and he led the flock to the far side of the wilderness and came to Horeb, the mountain of God. There the angel of the LORD appeared to him in flames of fire from within a bush.

— Exodus 3:1–2a

Reflection:

The desert! Of all the places and of all the ways imaginable, the *Lord appeared* to Moses in the desert. That's the way I always looked at this passage. But then it occurred to me, what if it read like this: "Moses was in the desert when he *noticed* that the Lord had appeared to him." That completely changed the emphasis of the passage for me. But either way, Moses encountered God in the desert, so when I needed divine direction, I headed out into the scorching July heat to seek God in the desert.

I had started a ministry at Epworth by the Sea on St. Simons Island called Adventure Ministries. It took off and quickly reached the point of my initial vision, and while I knew there was more to come, I didn't know what it was or what needed to happen next. So, I headed out with a few friends to the Utah desert determined to hear God's voice on what I called "The Great Vision Quest."

We biked the Slick Rock Trail, climbed mountains, and stood in awe of the vast expanse of creation. I expected grand revelations—maybe even a "burning bush" moment—but instead, I found something subtler and deeper.

Sitting under the vast Utah sky one night, staring at the stars and sheer cliffs, I realized just how small I was. Up to this point in my journey, I mistakenly had seen myself as… well, as kind of a big deal. Now for the first time, I saw myself clearly: unneeded in God's grand design and yet deeply loved. God didn't need me to accomplish His plans, but He wanted me to participate because of His love. I didn't come away from that trip with a clear vision for the next season of Adventure Ministries, but I had a deep assurance that what needed to happen had happened. Perhaps even more importantly, I had a better understanding of my relationship with God. He loves me! He has invited me to join in His work not because He needs me but because I am very special to Him.

We just need to slow down and notice.

Moses was in the wilderness tending sheep when he noticed the burning bush. It wasn't unusual for bushes to catch fire in the desert, but Moses paused and looked closer. That pause changed everything.

Like Moses, we often rush through life, missing the signs of God's presence in our busyness. The bush wasn't extraordinary—it was Moses' attention that made it holy.

If we learn to slow down and pay attention, we'll discover that God is constantly speaking, not in booming voices or flashing signs but in the everyday hum of life. God doesn't need us to do more; He invites us to see more, hear more, and trust that He's always near.

Reflection Question:

Where in your daily routine might God be inviting you to slow down and notice Him?

Prayer:

Lord, open my eyes to see you in the ordinary moments of my day. Teach me to pause, notice, and respond to your presence. Help me to trust that you are always near, speaking through the simple things around me. Amen.

Day 3: God Woos

Key Concept:

God wants to get our attention.

Scripture:

Now Moses was tending the flock of Jethro his father-in-law, the priest of Midian, and he led the flock to the far side of the wilderness and came to Horeb, the mountain of God. There the angel of the LORD appeared to him in flames of fire from within a bush. Moses saw that though the bush was on fire it did not burn up.
— Exodus 3:1–2

Reflection:

God caught Moses attention with a "burning bush" that did not burn out. We will think more about the bush in days to come but today let's take time to notice what God is doing here. He is getting Moses' attention. He is drawing Moses to Him. He is piquing Moses' curiosity to put him in a teachable posture.

My son, Cole, recently got married to Bailey. She has unquestionably, officially become the greatest gift giver in our family, but when the kids were growing up, I was repeatedly crowned as the king gift giver. Each birthday or Christmas, the kids would get very excited over my gift to them. They would love it more than any other gift, and their enthusiasm showed. In fact, it showed so much my wife started getting a bit frustrated because it happened every time. She actually gave much better gifts than me. She spent way more time thinking about what to get each child. She spent far more time shopping for them, and she spent far more money than me, but they always loved my gift more.

Finally, my wife, Kim, came to me and asked, "How do you do it?"

"How do I do what?" I asked.

She said, "How do you always manage to get the kids exactly what they want?"

I laughed and said, "Honey, I don't get the kids what they want. I get the kids to want what I have gotten them."

I have listened to a lot of sermons over the years, and many of them are theologically solid and totally true. Unfortunately, they are often answering questions no one is asking.

If the key to great gift giving is getting people to want what you have gotten them, then the key to great communication is getting people to ask the questions you are about to answer. That is what God does. He woos us. He gets our attention and draws us closer. He creates in us a thirst, a hunger, and a discontent which only He can satisfy.

We don't notice normal things. You ride to work the same way each day, and you pass the same house on the same streets, and nothing stands out to you. You arrive at work and probably can't even remember anything about any of the houses you past or even that you passed them. But if one of them was on fire on the morning you happened to drive past, you would notice. It would capture your attention.

God often uses odd, unusual, or out of the ordinary things to woo us. Charlie Walker was a teacher at my jr. high school. He wasn't a coach; he was a teacher. I never had him for a class and actually don't even know what he taught. The only thing I initially knew about him was he loved Jesus more than most people I knew. I mean this guy was totally sold out to following God and that caught my attention. He loved God, and he loved people in a way that was inspiring, so we started hanging out. As our friendship grew and deepened, others started coming and hanging out with us. At first, it was his passion which caught my attention. It was clear he really believed this stuff, and the way he lived every aspect of his life proved it. But here is the thing, he started a ministry with a group of kids called "First Love Ministries" that is still touching kids' lives almost 50 years later.

God is wooing us. He wants us to draw near to Him, and He will often use things which at first glance may seem out of the ordinary, odd, or even wrong to get our attention. Don't be too quick to jump to conclusions. Be curious. God might just be trying to get you to ask the question He is about to answer for you.

Reflection Question:

How might God be wooing you today to draw closer and become more curious?

Prayer:

Lord, you are with me, but I am often blinded by distractions. Help me to notice you today. Help me to be curious about what you are doing in and around me today. May your Spirit guide my steps and give me the courage to join with you in whatever you are doing. Amen.

Day 4: Moses Responds

Key Concept:

God initiates our response.

Scripture:

So Moses thought, "I will go over and see this strange sight—why the bush does not burn up."

— Exodus 3:3

Reflection:

God invites us into a relationship with Him, and as we will see in days to come, He offers us an opportunity to be a part of what He is doing. However, that requires a response on our part. God doesn't just force us to do things. Our whole spiritual journey is really a call and response journey. To lay a foundation for how important the order is, here is an outline of the call and response of Moses' calling:

God got Moses a job with Jethro **vs 1** Moses shows up at work **vs 2** God woos **vs 3** Moses notices **vs 4** God calls. Moses comes **vs 5–9** God reveals: Moses listens & learns **vs 10** God sends **vs 11** Moses doubts **vs 12** God reminds

The pattern we need to pay attention to is that God's initiation requires a response on our part. I believe it was Eddie Fox and George Morrison who said, "To preach and not present the Gospel is a sin and to preach the Gospel and not call for a response is a sin."

God honors our small, faith-filled steps. I know this to be true. Looking back, I see clearly how small and insignificant my steps of faith have been. By that I mean, knowing what I know now, seeing how it all played out, they were no brainer steps. Looking in the rear view mirror, I am so glad I took each one and would do so a million times again. Yet, God doesn't ask me to take those steps again because now they require no faith. Now, He is calling me to take new steps, which, when they are in front of me, seem so huge and risky, so scary.

Many of the steps God has historically called me to take to join Him in what He was doing were into big things, exciting new ventures—launching ministries, planting churches, birthing global denominations. It seems He has me moving in a different direction now, a direction for which I feel far less equipped to handle, which might be the point.

Margaret Mead was a famous anthropologist who was asked by a student what she considered to be the first sign of civilization in a culture. Much to everyone's surprise, Dr. Mead's answer was skeletal remains of people who had broken femurs that had later healed. Her point was that in uncivilized cultures or in the wild, a broken femur was a death sentence. They would be defenseless and helpless to fend off predators. They had to have someone who cared enough to protect and provide for them until they could heal. Living for the sake of others is the mark of true love and the mark of a civilized culture.

Last weekend, Kim and I moved out of the house we have lived in for the past two decades to move in with her mom, who fell and broke her femur. This is a new chapter in our lives, and it has put me in a great place, back on my knees crying out to God for help.

God doesn't need us to accomplish His plans. He includes us in what He is doing because it is how He plans on growing us. My friend and spiritual mentor, Tom Tanner, gave me some great advice years ago when he said, "Look for where God is moving and then do whatever you have to do to get there with Him." I might add "and if it takes you into waters that are over your head, even better."

Reflection Question:

How is God wanting you to respond to what He has been doing?

Prayer:

Lord, forgive me for making excuses and focusing on the wrong direction. I know what you are calling me to do, but I need your Spirit to enable me to have the faith to follow through. Help me take a step today. Amen.

Day 5: Lasting Burn

Key Concept:

We need consistency over intensity.

Scripture:

So Moses thought, "I will go over and see this strange sight—why the bush does not burn up."

— Exodus 3:3

Reflection:

Growing up, my father would never let me win at anything. Not that he was cruel, he just didn't let me win. He would handicap himself in some way to even the playing field, and then he would do his best, or at least what seemed like his best, to win. He might play me standing on one foot or only using his left hand, but with his limitation, he would play to win. I would typically get out to a quick lead, but as he adjusted to his handicap and I became overconfident, he would generally close the gap and in the last moment take the lead and snatch victory from defeat. Then he would say, "Son, stamina and experience will always prevail over youthful enthusiasm."

I still remember those games, and I still remember the wisdom of his logic.

In the long run, it is only those that finish the race that even have a chance to win. I've seen a lot of impressive starts to the Christian journey that ended up only flashes in the pan. Obviously, this is unfortunate for the person involved, but I think it is also unfortunate for the entire Christian community. Most of our "burning bushes" will be people who are on fire for the Lord. God uses the lives of others to catch our attention. He uses them to draw us into a personal conversation with Him. Those who quickly catch our attention in a bright flash of flare, only to just as abruptly crash, disillusion and discourage us.

But the life lived well over the long haul is the legend that leads us to a personal encounter with God. We are drawn to consistency, to the flame that doesn't go out. We want to know how and why it continues to burn because we also want to be consumed by a fire that doesn't burn out.

Moses didn't just glance at the burning bush and move on. He stopped, looked closer, and lingered long enough to notice that something was unusual. That act of paying attention opened the door to a divine encounter that would change the course of history.

There's something captivating about a sustained burn. It's not just a flash of brilliance but a steady, ongoing flame. That's what draws us in: consistency over time. Just as my dad used to tell me during our games, stamina and experience are what will last—not enthusiasm. His wisdom holds true in faith as well: a life well-lived for the long haul leaves a legacy that inspires others to listen for God.

It has been said burnout happens when we lose sight of why we're doing what we do, and I believe that is true. However, I have noticed my campfire burns out not because it has forgotten its purpose, but because I haven't continued to put logs on the fire. I think many people burn out simply because they have not implemented a plan to live for the long haul. Like a campfire, our lives need fuel. We must nurture the flame with the discipline of listening and watching for God in the everyday. God's voice often comes not in spectacular displays but in the steady presence of His love, sustaining us over time.

Reflection Question:

What "strange sights" or consistent burns in your life might God be using to capture your attention?

Prayer:

Lord, help me to slow down and notice your steady presence in my life. Teach me to recognize the extraordinary in the ordinary and to trust that you are working in the long haul. Amen.

Day 6: Practical Application: Creating Space to Hear

Key Concept:

Cultivate habits of listening to God.

Action Step:

Before moving on, reflect and act on the following:

1. Identify one area in your daily life where you can slow down to notice God's presence.

2. Develop your own Spiritual Rule, a plan for regularly creating space to listen to God. For example:

   - Spend time daily in scripture.

   - Practice silence and solitude.

   - Write down moments when you sense God speaking.

Create a dedicated time or space each day to listen to God. Use practical steps like journaling, removing distractions, or setting specific times for reflection.

Reflection Question:

What habits or routines might help you hear God more clearly in your everyday life?

Prayer:

Lord, give me the wisdom to create space for you in my life. Help me develop habits that draw me closer to you and allow me to hear your voice. Amen.

Day 7: Rest, Recap, & Reflect

Key Concept:

Take stock of what we've learned about listening.

Recap:

This week, we explored the beginnings of listening to God. We saw Moses' example of paying attention to the ordinary and discovered that God's voice is always near, inviting us to notice and respond. We've reflected on creating space for God, clearing distractions, and being present in the moment.

As you move forward, remember: God is speaking to you, even in the smallest details of your life. The journey of listening begins with slowing down, noticing, and trusting.

Reflection Questions:

What moments this week helped you notice God's presence?

What habits or practices will you commit to for better listening in the coming week?

What do you think God might be trying to say to you?

How do you think He might want you to respond?

Prayer:

Lord, thank you for showing me how to listen this week. Help me carry these lessons forward, creating space for you and trusting in your voice. Amen.

Week 2: God Calls.
Exodus 3:4–5

Theme:

God calls each of us, and we must learn to recognize and respond to His voice.

Introduction:

Once we've begun to quiet the noise and notice God's presence, the next step is learning to trust what we hear. Trusting the whisper of God's voice requires faith, humility, and an openness to act on what we hear.

Sometimes, God's voice comes gently, like a whisper in our spirit. At other times, it challenges us, asking us to let go of control and follow His lead. This week, we'll explore what it means to trust God's voice as it aligns with His character, His heart, and His plans.

As we journey together, remember that learning to trust takes time. God is patient with us, guiding us step by step. Our task is to listen, trust, and obey.

Day 8: God Sees

Key Concept:

God recognizes our effort.

Scripture:

When the LORD *saw that he had gone over to look . . .*
— Exodus 3:4a

Reflection:

God got Moses' attention. Moses responded by coming closer, and God noticed Moses' response. What we will see happen next is God calling Moses by name and eventually including him in an adventure that changes the trajectory of history. But what if Moses had not recognized the voice of God?

Henry Blackaby points out in *Experiencing God* that if we are not able to hear and recognize the voice of God we have a critical flaw in our spiritual development. Hearing and recognizing the voice of God is essential to being a follower of Christ. So why do so few people feel like they are able to hear God?

Too many Christians today don't believe God is talking to them, so obviously, they don't invest time or energy in listening. Not believing leads to not listening. Not listening leads to not hearing. Not hearing leads to not obeying. Not obeying leads to not becoming more like Christ. Less Christians conforming to the image of Christ leads to more Christians who are not Christ-like, which means a world who really needs to see Jesus is not getting a good picture of who He really is. Not hearing God is a serious problem with significant consequences.

So how can you and I start doing a better job hearing what God is trying to say to us?

The clear first step is to begin to believe God is actually speaking to us. God is talking to you. He has things He wants you to know, and He has things He wants you to do, and He is trying to convey those things to you. He is talking to you through the Spirit, through the Bible, through others, through circumstances, through nature, through your mind, through your emotions. God has more languages than we can imagine. The breakdown in communication is not on His end; it is on ours. We will not seriously begin to listen until we are convinced God is trying to communicate with us.

The second necessary step is cultivating a rhythm of silence and solitude in our routine. God certainly doesn't only speak to us when we're quiet and alone, but it is in these times that we learn to discern or recognize the voice of God. When we have a regular pattern of listening, hearing, and recognizing God in the silence and solitude, we can then pick up His voice in the crowd and chaos of life. If we have not cultivated that gift in private, it will not work in public.

The third essential step is living in an authentic community. Community not only helps us accurately understand what God is actually saying to us, it also enables us to consistently obey Him. The more we accurately respond to God's voice, the better our hearing becomes, and vice versa, when we fail to respond to God's call on our lives, we begin to lose our ability to hear and recognize His voice.

Listening isn't a passive activity; it requires intentionality. Busyness and distractions are some of the greatest obstacles to hearing God. When we don't intentionally slow down, we can miss His voice altogether. To start listening, we must create space for silence and be willing to let go of preconceived notions about what God might say.

Moses didn't decide what the burning bush should mean—he simply noticed it and paid attention. We can start listening in the same way: by slowing down, clearing the noise, and being open to hearing God in unexpected ways.

Reflection Question:

What steps can you take this week to clear distractions and start listening to God?

Prayer:

Lord, give me the courage to slow down and be still before you. Help me to trust that you are speaking and to approach your voice with openness and humility. Amen.

Day 9: God Calls his Name

Key Concept:

God meets us in the present moment and calls us by name.

Scripture:

When the LORD saw that he had gone over to look, God called to him from within the bush, "Moses! Moses!"

— Exodus 3:4a

Reflection:

I once didn't hire a guy because he walked too slowly. I tend to move fast and like to get things done. The more plates spinning, the better, and the closer to the deadline, the more adrenalin I get. Productivity is important. Yet as I look back, by far the most impactful moments of my life were when, at least for a moment, I slowed down, and time stopped. It was in those moments when the distractions faded, and I was able to be fully present that profound things happened.

When my son Cole was perhaps three or four, he was the resident theologian in our house. Each morning, I would get up and start the mad rush of the day. As I would quickly grab something to eat and head out the door to go to work, he would often send me out with a cheerful, "Tell them about Jesus! Daddy, tell them about Jesus!"

One day, I must not have been in the ordinary rush, so I thought I would see if there was really anything to Cole's morning declarations or if he was just parroting something he had heard. I decided to test him a bit. As I prepared to leave, right on queue, Cole cheered, "Tell them about Jesus! Daddy, tell them about Jesus!"

So, I stopped, look down at him, and gently asked, "Do you know where Jesus is?"

Without a moment's hesitation, he replied, "Sure I do, Dad!" Thinking he was going to say something like in heaven or in the sky, I asked him where he thought Jesus was, and he looked me square in the eye and said, "He is in you, Daddy!"

God didn't need me to raise Cole; I needed Cole to help me become more like Christ.

God doesn't need us to accomplish His plans. He includes us in His plans to complete us, to grow us, to help us become more like Jesus for the sake of others.

Too often we miss what God is doing because we live in the past or the future, replaying regrets or planning what's next. But God calls us to the present where He is actively working. The burning bush didn't appear in Moses' past or future; it appeared right where he was in the middle of his ordinary day.

Being present means resisting the urge to rush or multitask and instead focusing fully on the moment. It's about noticing God's presence here and now, trusting that He is near and ready to speak.

What would change in your life if you approached each moment as a chance to encounter God?

Reflection Question:

How can you practice being fully present today to notice God's work around you?

Prayer:

Lord, help me to be present in this moment and to trust that you are here with me. Teach me to listen and respond to your voice in the here and now. Amen.

Day 10: The Correct Response

Key Concept:

God's call requires our response.

Scripture:

When the LORD saw that he had gone over to look, God called to him from within the bush, "Moses! Moses!" And Moses said, "Here I am."

— Exodus 3:4

Reflection:

What a perfect response from Moses, "Here I am." "I am" and "I am not" will play a big role in this conversation, but Moses introduces the phrase here as the perfect statement of fact to God calling out his name. He does not add any evaluation to the fact like Peter did on the Mount of Transfiguration when he said, "It is good for us to be here" (Matthew 17:4a), nor does he jump to take action like Peter saying, "How about I build a shelter?" Moses simply says "Here I am." Perhaps Moses thought God calling his name was a question, as in "where are you," and his reply was "I am right here." Or maybe Moses thought God's calling his name was a command to come here, and his reply was meant to indicate "I am here."

Whatever the case, it sounds a lot like Samuel saying, "Speak, for your servant is listening" (1 Samuel 3:10b), which I believe is the correct response to every encounter with God and the heart of what I am hoping to get at through these devotions. We tend to "do" too much for God and are seldom just fully present with Him. Thus, we don't hear God consistently.

My friend, Steve Lane, who is now a Christian missionary in Utah was once on the USA bobsledding team. What makes that hilarious is that we lived on a coastal island in South Georgia where not only did it never really snow but also the biggest hill was the bridge onto the island. He was a man of strong faith, and I felt like this bobsledding thing could be a great platform for him to utilize to do some speaking around the country. When I pitched the idea to him, he wasn't interested at all. When I questioned him about not wanting to do the speaking circuit, his reply was years ahead of its time. He said, speaking is not where things really happen, small groups is. Let's put our effort into small groups. Later, after the small group movement had really become the in thing, I ran into him and asked how his small groups were going, and he said, "Oh, small groups is not where it is happening. It is one-on-one ministry that makes the biggest impact."

He had a lot of wisdom. I spend a lot of time in one-on-one relationships, but I still also do a good amount of work with small groups. I will on occasion do a small group that is based on some content or curriculum, but by far my favorite format for ministry, be it one on one or small group, is to ask three simple questions which I think are the key to life and ministry.

1. What do you think God might possibly be trying to say to you?

I like stating it this way because it leans heavily away from "Thus saith the Lord." I much prefer, "I am not sure, but it seems like God might be trying to tell me _____." This invites Christian conferencing and conversation for greater clarity and discernment. It also keeps me in a posture of openness and curiosity.

2. How do you think God might want you to respond?

God speaking is always an invitation to respond in some form or fashion. The response is not necessarily an action or even anything to "do" but may be an invitation to "do less" or "be more."

3. How can we help you?

This question lets them know they are not alone in this, and none of us are called to travel our spiritual journeys in isolation. We need each other in order to consistently, faithfully follow Christ.

Reflection Question:

God is calling your name. He does it every day. Can you honestly reply, "Here I am, Lord"? What could you do now to be more fully present with God?

Prayer:

Here I am. Speak Lord, for your servant is listening. Amen.

Day 11: God Commands

Key Concept:

God's commandments are for our ultimate good and His ultimate Glory.

Scripture:

"Do not come any closer," God said. *"Take off your sandals . . ."*
— Exodus 3:5a

Reflection:

Wait what? Do not come any closer? You called me. Why would God call Moses to come closer and then command him to stop? I am sure there are biblical scholars who could take us on a deep dive into the holiness of God, and I am sure I would completely agree with their explanation of this sudden shift in tone and direction. However, my experience has been God operates on multiple layers simultaneously. For instance, this whole thing He is setting up with Moses to deliver His people from slavery and take them through the wilderness into the promised land is simultaneously an actual historic event and a metaphor for all our spiritual journeys. God is calling Moses, but He is also revealing how He calls each of us.

Remember my teacher friend Charlie Walker, who I introduced you to a few days ago? Well, his passion for Christ got me passionate about fully following God no matter what He called me to do. I got really serious about my faith. Up until this time I was only serious about sports, baseball in particular. I wasn't really big or fast, but I had this uncanny ability to hit a baseball a long way. My previous season had gone very well, and I had caught the attention of the baseball coaches. I was also the starting quarterback for the football team, but my baseball skills were my strong suit. I really enjoyed playing, and I really liked the coach.

So, it was a hard pill to swallow when I felt God was calling me not to play baseball. It made no sense, but I knew God was telling me not to play. Telling my coach was going to be really hard; he would not understand this at all. When I told him, he asked me why I wasn't going to play, and I made up a story about needing to get a job. He said he could hire me to clean up some stuff around the gym so I could play. Then I had to tell him I felt like God told me not to play. He didn't understand, I didn't understand, and neither one of us was happy about it.

A few other things happened in the years to come which disappointed me and which I allowed to get between me and God. For a long time, I was mad because I felt like God asked me to do some things that just didn't make sense. Some people probably thought I misunderstood God or was completely off in my thinking, but I was and am still convinced God told me not to play, even though for decades I never understood why. I wondered if He knew I was going to be injured if I played and was thus keeping me from getting hurt. We did go on to win the National Championship in football, so maybe He was closing the baseball door to take me in that direction but that didn't feel right either.

Eventually I got over my anger and got back on track with God. A few years ago, I was spending time with God praying, and I just asked, "God, why in the world did you tell me to stop playing baseball?"

Maybe I am still off and perhaps none of it was God, but I think God said, "Jay, I had great plans for big things which I wanted to include you in, but in order to do so, I had to know you were going to do what I said even when you didn't understand or like it." WOW! I sure am glad I listened to God and did what He said.

Reflection Question:

How do you respond when God isn't doing what you want Him to do?

Prayer:

Lord, help me trust in you. Not simply trust what you say but trust you. Trust you no matter what you say, no matter what you do or don't do. Help me to know you so intimately that I trust you completely. Amen.

Day 12: Walking on Holy Ground

Key Concept:

God transforms the ordinary into the extraordinary.

Scripture:

"Do not come any closer," God said. *"Take off your sandals, for the place where you are standing is holy ground."*

— Exodus 3:5

Reflection:

Can you imagine hearing God declare that the very place upon which you stood was holy ground? The awe. The amazement. The fear. The confusion?

"Wait a minute; I'm pretty sure this is the same place I camped last spring. Yeah, I found a stray sheep right over there one time. I have been past this spot a hundred times in the past 40 years, and I never heard that it was 'holy ground.'"

What makes it so holy now?

Moses had likely walked past that spot countless times, yet on this day, it became sacred—not because the place had changed but because God's presence was there, and Moses noticed.

We often dismiss ordinary places and moments in our lives. But when we slow down and become aware of God's presence, we realize that He is with us everywhere, turning the mundane into holy ground.

I was leading a Methodist Men's retreat, and they were notoriously rather slow. My role was simply to make sure they had everything they needed and to handle any problems that arose. The first meeting had just started, and I had settled into my chair in the back of the room to read while the session drew to a close. Although I was admittedly not paying full attention, I did notice when the speaker got up. He quickly rattled off this prayer, "Lord, do with me today whatever you must that in the future you may do with me whatever you wish." He had my fully attention—not the speaker, God.

"Lord, do with me today whatever you must that in the future you may do with me whatever you wish." What a powerful, profound prayer. Right there in the middle of the same old, same old, God appeared and spoke to me. I could not stop pondering that prayer, and I decided to start praying it daily. Becoming open to God working in me led me to begin to view everything that was happening to me not as normal, everyday life but as God's directing me, leading me to where He wanted me. That single "burning bush" moment began a period of preparation for me that is still unfolding today.

I've seen this transformation in my own life—whether in a small group in my basement or in a bowling alley that became a place of worship. It's not about the location; it's about God showing up and us being ready to listen.

Reflection Question:

Where might God be inviting you to take off your shoes and recognize holy ground in your life?

Prayer:

Lord, teach me to see your presence in the everyday places of my life. Help me to approach these moments with reverence, knowing that wherever you are, it is holy ground. Amen.

Day 13: Practical Application: Aligning Your Heart

Key Concept:

Reflect on and act in trust.

Action Step:

Take time today to reflect on what God has been speaking to you about this week. Write down:

1. One way you've seen His character revealed.
2. One area where your heart has been shaped by His.
3. One plan or decision where you need to trust Him more.

Examine areas where your plans may not align with God's. Include journaling prompts or questions about surrendering control and trusting in God's bigger picture.

Reflection Question:

What step can you take today to grow in trusting God's voice?

Prayer:

Lord, thank you for speaking to me this week. Help me to trust you more deeply and to take the next step of obedience. Amen.

Day 14: Rest, Recap, & Reflect

Key Concept:

Trust grows as we listen, believe, and obey.

Recap:

This week, we've explored what it means to trust the whisper of God's voice. We've reflected on His character, allowed His heart to shape ours, and considered how to align our plans with His. Along the way, we've faced doubts and learned the value of listening before acting.

Trust isn't built in an instant; it grows through daily choices to listen, believe, and obey. As you move forward, remember that God's whisper is always true, and His plans are always good.

Reflection Questions:

How has God's character encouraged you to trust His voice this week?

What step of trust do you feel God is inviting you to take next?

Prayer:

Lord, thank you for teaching me to trust you this week. Help me to carry these lessons forward, leaning on your strength and following your voice. Amen.

Week 3: God Reveals.
Exodus 3:6–9

Theme:

God reveals Himself and His plan as we begin to understand His will.

Introduction:

On a beach, a young child, his older brother, and their father and grandfather spent hours building a beautiful sandcastle. As the tide rushed in to destroy their creation, the youngest child lost interest and played with the dog, while the teenager built walls, dug motes, and fought to protect his work. Resigned to the inevitable, the grandfather watched undisturbed as the ocean swallowed the castle. But the father, realizing how important this was to his family, took a picture, preserving the sandcastle and the memories forever. I pray that God will keep us from losing interest, from fighting to save what should be lost, and from giving up, and I pray He will help us preserve what really matters. We've learned to listen to God and to trust His voice. Now, we must develop a proper perspective, cultivate a heart like God's, and understand His plan so that we may join with Him in what He is doing in our lives and our world.

Day 15: Developing the Proper Perspective

Key Concept:

Trust begins with knowing who God is.

Scripture:

Then he said, "I am the God of your father, the God of Abraham, the God of Isaac and the God of Jacob." At this, Moses hid his face, because he was afraid to look at God.

— Exodus 3:6

Reflection:

The first thing God reveals to Moses is who He is. Before asking Moses to act, God introduced Himself. He reminded Moses of His identity as the God of Abraham, Isaac, and Jacob—a God of covenant and faithfulness. This revelation from God is important. God wants Moses to understand who He is because a correct understanding of who God is gives Moses the proper perspective to see that the call wasn't about Moses' ability but about God's character.

During my "Hanson hinney hawler" days when I would take Cole and Summer to school, we developed this little ritual we would do on the drive:

I would cheerfully shout, "Have a great day!" and then deeply and boldly I ask, "And what is the way to have a great day?"

To which they would dutifully reply, "Make the best of it!"

"And how do you make the best of it?" I would then inquire.

"By having a good attitude!" they would scream.

"And what is the key to a good attitude?" I would immediately fire back.

"KEEPING A PROPER PERSEPECTIVE!" they shouted.

Then after a brief pause, I slowly and seriously asked, "And what is the proper perspective?"

To which we all boldly proclaimed, "TO ALWAYS REMEMBER THAT GOD LOVES ME AND DADDY DOES TOOOOOO!"

Developing and maintaining proper perspective is essential. Nothing can get you off course and in a ditch quicker than losing your perspective. God didn't want Moses to rush off into action, trusting in his own abilities. God wanted to lay a foundation in the heart of Moses that was built on the timeless character of God.

When a few of us began to respond to God's call on our lives, huddled together in my basement, our burning bush, the temptation was to rush into what we were to do. But what was our role? We knew something was happening, and we suspected it was going to be something new, but God had to teach us that what was happening was not something new but was simply another chapter in a story that has been unfolding for all of eternity. He didn't need us to do anything. He just wanted us to sit around the burning bush until we began to understand a little more fully who He was, is, and always will be…because He knew it would give us the proper perspective to start learning about His heart.

Understanding the character and nature of God and His faithfulness, love, and power helps us be able to respond with confidence, even when the path ahead is unclear. Like Moses, we might feel unqualified or afraid, but God's character assures us that He will equip and sustain us.

Reflection Question:

What aspects of God's character give you confidence to trust His voice?

Prayer:

Lord, help me to know you more deeply. Reveal your faithfulness and love so I can trust you with every part of my life. Amen.

Day 16: God Knows

Key Concept:

We begin to grasp what moves the heart of God.

Scripture:

The LORD said, "I have indeed seen the misery of my people in Egypt. I have heard them crying out because of their slave drivers, and I am concerned about their suffering.

— Exodus 3:7

Reflection:

After God reveals His character to Moses by letting him know who He has been, is, and always will be, God begins to reveal His heart to Moses. God knows that for Moses to become the leader God plans for him to be, Moses will need to understand the heart of God and learn to care about the things which God cares about. God reveals three things which each point to the condition of His heart: what He sees, what He hears, and what concerns Him.

God says, "I have indeed seen the misery of my people in Egypt." He is saying I am aware of what is going on. I know you are hurting. I see you. I have not forsaken you. I am not in the dark, and I have not forgotten about you. Suffering is hard enough no matter the circumstances, but when you feel all alone and as if no one sees your pain, it makes the suffering that much more unbearable.

It had been one of those weeks. Actually, it had been years of hard stuff on top of hard stuff. The challenges of this week just made me a little less apt at concealing the inner struggle. I was doing so badly I didn't even realize how much it was showing.

The Wednesday night ministries were in full swing at the Chapel. There were groups gathering in every room we had, and some young ladies were even meeting out on the porch. As I was moving from one building to another, Kayla called out to me from the porch with the customary "how's it going?" I don't exactly know how I responded, but my attempt to suggest everything was okay and move on to the next thing didn't fly with Kayla. She responded to my reply with a clearly sarcastic, "Well, that was really believable." Her tone was not critical or judgmental. It was an invitation to be honest.

So, I stopped, turned to walk toward the group of ladies, and simply told the truth. "I am having a bad day. Things are getting to me more than normal, and I am not doing well." I tried not to sound like I was complaining or to imply that I didn't know the tide would turn. I asked her if she was familiar with the singer Jelly Roll, which she was not. "He has a song," I said, "Which says 'I am not okay, but everything is going to be alright.' That is my theme song these days."

Kayla handled it perfectly. She didn't minimize my struggle. She didn't try to correct my thinking or fix my problems. She did something far better. She said, "Just know I see you. I see your struggle." Again, she wasn't being judgmental or critical, she was just letting me know I am not alone, and I found comfort in knowing there are lots of people who see me, they get me, they understand what I am going through, and they are pulling for me.

All of us are either coming out of, in the middle of, or heading into struggles. Hard times are an unavoidable part of life in our fallen state. However, we also have a Heavenly Father, who is always either preparing us for, walking with us in, or guiding us out of struggles. Knowing God sees us where we are is a source of comfort for many of us.

Yet, there are those who have a very different gut reaction to hearing, "God sees you." When you don't have an accurate understanding of the true nature of God, it can invoke fear in your soul to know that God is fully aware of your state. When you don't know His heart or how He feels about you, it can be scary to know He sees you. I am hoping in the days to come as God continues to reveal His heart to us, you will begin to experience how much God loves you and how much He is for you.

Reflection Question:

How does the fact that God sees you impact you? Why?

Prayer:

Psalm 139:23–24: "Search me, God, and know my heart; test me and know my anxious thoughts. See if there is any offensive way in me, and lead me in the way everlasting." Amen.

Day 17: God Hears

Key Concept:

God hears our tears.

Scripture:

The LORD said, "I have indeed seen the misery of my people in Egypt. I have heard them crying out because of their slave drivers, and I am concerned about their suffering."

— Exodus 3:7

Reflection:

God sees our struggles, and He hears our tears. Our crying out to God is not pointless. He hears our prayers, and His answer is always what is ultimately best for us. There is the tension point for me though—"ultimately best." I often don't want "ultimately best;" I want "immediate relief."

Just as I am still learning to listen to God, prayer is another thing I'm growing in.

On the one hand, it is the single most amazing thing about God to me. The big stuff doesn't impress me. So, Jesus walked on water; God created the oceans. Walking on water isn't that big a deal if you are God. Jesus raised people from the dead. God is the source of all life; of course, Jesus can call Lazarus out of a tomb. Jesus fed 5,000 men, but God feeds the whole world every day. God spoke the universe into being. Read the last part of Job, and you'll begin to see how huge God is and how powerful He is. I get it. He is a big deal, and there is nothing He can't do.

Here is what gets me. That great, big, huge God, the creator of the universe, knows my name and He hears me when I pray. Can you image that? With everything that is happening and with everyone who is praying, God can still hear and recognize my heart crying out to Him. That is mind boggling.

On the other hand, if He loves me and hears me, why isn't He answering my prayers? Why is my wife still totally blind in one eye? Why does my son still have seizures? Why do the people I love still not follow Christ?

Cole had his first brain surgery when he was one. Everything went just like the doctors said it would. They found what they thought they would find. They did what they planned to do, and they said it went just like they expected it would. I was ticked! I was so mad I ran out of the hospital. I was mad because it seemed like God didn't do anything.

For quite some time after that, God and I had some heated conversations, which eventually ended up sounding a little like God's response to Job: "Then the LORD spoke to Job out of the storm. He said: 'Who is this that obscures my plans with words without knowledge? Brace yourself like a man; I will question you, and you shall answer me. 'Where were you when I laid the earth's foundation? Tell me, if you understand'" (Job 38:1–4).

Specifically, this is what I felt God was saying to me: "Jay, you misunderstand the point of prayer and thus the very nature of our relationship. The point of prayer is to help you learn to trust my heart. You need to know how our relationship works and then decide if you still want to follow me. You don't tell me what to do. I tell you what to do. I don't not do what you tell me to do because I am cruel but because I know better than you. I will always do what is right and best, whether you like it or not."

God made it clear how our relationship worked, and the important role prayer plays in it. Prayer was not a technique I could use to get what I wanted but a path to help me get in step with what God was doing. I decided then and there I was all in with God and would trust Him over my skewed and limited understanding.

Reflection Question:

What is your understanding of the purpose of prayer in your relationship with God?

Prayer:

Lord, help me put prayer in the proper place in my life, and teach me to pray the way you want me to pray and for the things for which you want me to pray. Help me to learn to trust you. Amen.

Day 18: God Cares

Key Concept:

Trusting God means allowing His passions to shape ours.

Scripture:

The LORD said, "I have indeed seen the misery of my people in Egypt. I have heard them crying out because of their slave drivers, and I am concerned about their suffering."

— Exodus 3:7

Reflection:

I remember the first time I came across Bob Pierce's quote, "Let my heart be broken by the things that break the heart of God." It was on page 132 of *Experiencing God* among a list of other incredible quotes from famous missionaries. His saying just jumped out and grabbed me. I immediately began to write it down and thought, 'I want this to be my prayer.' But then mid-sentence it hit me.

God's heart was broken by losing His son.

At the time, my son, Cole, had just recovered from brain surgery, and the thought of losing him was unbearable. I wrote, "I cannot do it God; I am simply not prepared to handle the pain of having a heart that feels what you feel."

About seven years later, my son had complications with his shunt, and our medical nightmares returned. Hospital after hospital, test after test, and they still refused to listen to us. Finally, we had more surgery, only to have additional complications follow.

The single instance most accurately encapsulating the entire experience was when they finally tapped Cole's shunt. After repeated efforts, our neurosurgeon finally agreed to stick a needle into Cole's head to measure the pressure and see if his shunt had malfunctioned. He calmly assured Cole it wouldn't hurt. Then I held Cole down as I whispered, "This won't hurt a bit." As the doctor stuck the huge needle into Cole's head, it hurt, Cole flinched, and the needle came out, so the doctor jabbed it quickly back in causing incredible pain.

The needle is attached to a beaker, which catches the brain fluid that flows into it. Depending on the amount of pressure in the brain, the fluid level will rise to a marked number. Cole's pressure was so high that the fluid literally spewed out of the beaker and splashed on the ceiling. I looked on in horror, seeing Cole's tear-filled eyes as he said, "YOU SAID IT WOULDN'T HURT. I WILL NEVER TRUST YOU AGAIN."

To Cole, I was the source of his pain. I was the one who held him down every time he was poked and prodded. I was the one who took him to places where he didn't want to go. I was the one who said it was going to get better when it hadn't and who said it wouldn't hurt when it did. He became very angry with me, and I became very angry with God.

Abby Downing, one of the significant seven who began praying in my basement for what eventually became The Chapel, came to see me and told me she felt like she had a word from God for me. She said, "God loves you enough to do for you what you need, even if it makes you mad." I just cried. Just like Cole couldn't understand that everything I did was out of love for him, I couldn't understand how God was using all this for my ultimate good. He was teaching me what it feels like to have the heart of the Father. He was preparing me to have a pastor's heart for His people.

When God called Moses, He shared His heart for the Israelites' suffering. Before Moses could act, he needed to understand what moved God. Trusting God's voice involves allowing Him to shape our hearts, teaching us to care about what He cares about.

When we align our hearts with God's, we'll see the world through His eyes, moving in step with His Spirit.

Reflection Question:

What is God placing on your heart right now, and how can you respond?

Prayer:

Lord, break my heart for what breaks yours. Teach me to see the world through your eyes and trust your timing and ways. Amen.

Day 19: God Reveals His Plan

Key Concept:

Trusting God means aligning with His plans—not ours.

Scripture:

So I have come down to rescue them from the hand of the Egyptians and to bring them up out of that land into a good and spacious land, a land flowing with milk and honey . . .

— Exodus 3:8a

Reflection:

When I was about to graduate college, I took a career aptitude assessment. According to the assessment, I tended to make hasty decisions. I disagreed, but I decided to ask my dad. My dad and I talk while fishing, so as we fished from our canoe in a small pond, I explained how, while it might appear that I am rash, the truth is I think faster than others and have accurately considered all options. As I continued, I cast my line, and my pole snapped. My rod and reel went flying, but before they could fall and sink into the abyss, I stood up and dove out of the canoe, grabbing them midair. I fell into the water, only to stand and discover it was just a couple of feet deep. With my argument against rash choices still echoing, Dad just helped me back in the boat. Nothing needed to be said.

Gifted leaders struggle with trusting God because they think too highly of themselves and too little of God. They have been able to succeed, and this seduces them into relying on their own ability. I know I do this. Rather than starting out listening to God, I only turn to Him when I desperately need Him to show up.

Once I was scheduled to speak at Buckhorn Methodist Church. The only thing that is scarier than speaking to an uninterested crowd is speaking to an expectant crowd. I was gripped with uncertainty. As the date grew closer, I searched for something to say, but nothing came.

When the weekend came, I went to the church hours early with no clue what I would say. I walked, sat, thought, and prayed. I laid on the alter and cried, "Lord, YOUR people are going to fill this room expecting me to say something from you; I don't know what to do. What do you want me to do?" Then I stared at the ceiling, listening, and... I started counting ceiling tiles. I would begin to count, lose count, then try again until I lost my spot. I finally yelled, "Lord, you expect me to speak for you and I can't even count tiles!"

Then God said, "You see that one tile? Just worry about that one, and I will take care of the rest."

In other words, it's not up to me. I can't blow the deal, nor can I save the day. God has decided what He will do and nothing and no one can stop Him. My role is to seek God and share what He shows me.

Moses blew it the first time. He heard the Israelites' cry, saw the Egyptians mistreating them, and wanted to deliver them—a good thing, but he did it the wrong way at the wrong time. Moses got ahead of God.

Every coin has two sides, every strength a weakness. The passion, drive, and clarity of vision that make great leaders can also make them jump too soon. Trusting God's voice means surrendering our plans and aligning with His. It's tempting to forge ahead, but God's ways are higher than ours. When we listen and trust, we'll see Him accomplish things beyond imagination.

Reflection Question:

Where might God be asking you to set aside your plans to trust His?

Prayer:

Lord, help me to surrender my plans and align with yours. Teach me to trust that your ways are always best. Amen.

Day 20: Practical Application: Obeying the Call

Key Concept:

Reflect on and apply what God has spoken to you this week.

Action Step:

Take time today to reflect on the week's themes and put them into practice:

1. Identify one area where God is calling you to take action.
2. Write down one practical step of obedience you can take this week.
3. Share your step with someone who can pray for and encourage you.

Reflection Question:

How can you move from listening to action in your faith journey?

Prayer:

Lord, thank you for speaking to me this week. Help me to take the next step of obedience and to trust you in every part of my journey. Amen

Day 21: Rest, Recap, and Reflect

Key Concept:

Hearing God's voice leads to transformation and obedience.

Recap:

This week, we focused on moving from listening to action. We explored how God's presence equips us, how opposition strengthens our faith, and how trust in His timing leads to obedience.

God doesn't call us to stay where we are—He calls us to step forward in faith, trusting that He will guide and provide. As you reflect on this week, consider how God is inviting you to align your actions with His voice.

Reflection Questions:

What step of obedience has God called you to take this week?

How has your faith grown as you've trusted Him in action?

Prayer:

Lord, thank you for guiding me this week. Help me to continue stepping forward in obedience, trusting your presence and plan. Amen.

Week 4: God Sends.
Exodus 3:10–14

Theme:

God's "sending" is a call to "come" to Him.

Introduction:

In the NIV, vs10 starts with "So now, go." However, in the ESV, it begins "Come." God's call on our lives will always draw us closer to Him.

Following God's call always begins with listening before leaping. It will create real doubt which we wrestle with until we can depend on God and not ourselves. To do this consistently, we must have a personal relationship with God, so we can hear His whisper and know He is with us.

There are two equally deadly mistakes we can make in discerning our call. The first is to jump in too quickly, rather than listening first. The second is to think we are finished once we have done our part. The call always starts with listening, and it ends not by completing our task but by passing the baton to the next runner. The Christian journey is not a sprint but a relay race. Each runner runs their leg and then passes the mantle to the next generation.

Day 22: Listen Before Leaping

Key Concept:

Obedience begins with listening.

Scripture:

So now, go. I am sending you to Pharaoh to bring my people the Israelites out of Egypt.

— Exodus 3:10

Reflection:

As I write this chapter, I'm staying at a friend's cabin on Leatherwood Mountain in North Carolina. I have spent many hours walking in the woods. I haven't seen anyone in days and have been struck and disturbed by the silent stillness of this place. Nothing appears to be happening, yet I know it is. There are huge trees everywhere. They must be growing, but I cannot see or hear anything. There is evidence of activity everywhere, but none is seen. How long must it have taken for the trees to grow? Yet there is no rush here; everything that needs to happen seems to be happening. God's plan appears to be more slow and steady, more silent and stable, than my fast-paced, loud ways.

God didn't tell Moses to gather an army or even to grab a sword. He didn't develop a strategic plan or elaborate strategy. He simply said, "So go. Get my people." Discovering our call, our role, can be humbling, and it can be terrifying. On the one hand, Moses might have wanted a more prestigious appointment: troops to command, some demonstration of his importance. On the other hand, Pharaoh might just kill him.

When we view our part as just that—a part of what God IS doing—it keeps it in perspective. If we view it as independent or separate, the weight of responsibility would be crushing. A professor I once had said the burden of saving souls was why he didn't preach. My reply was that if I thought for a single second I was responsible for saving souls through my preaching, I wouldn't be able to bare the weight either, but when I understand that God is about to save souls, I race to see what He is doing.

One might ask, if God is going to do what He plans regardless, why does He utilize us in the process? The answer is because it is how He grows us. The basic difference between managing people and discipling them is that when you manage people, you use people to complete tasks. When you disciple people, you use tasks to develop people. God allows us to be a part of what He is doing not because He needs us but because we need Him. He builds our faith and perfects our character by allowing us to be a part of what He accomplishes. We miss many of the lessons because in our haste, we fail to take the time to observe and reflect. We rush from one task to the next and never ponder the point. We are missing our burning bushes because we aren't taking the time to notice the extraordinary in the ordinary.

Moses' calling began not with action but with listening. Before he could lead the Israelites, he had to hear God's voice, trust

His plan, and surrender his fears. Because we rush ahead, thinking we know best, we find ourselves frustrated or burned out. God's ways are not hurried; they are deliberate. Trusting His voice means pausing long enough to hear Him fully and align our actions with His will.

When I've rushed into action without listening, I've often ended up striving in my own strength. But when I've paused to hear God's voice, even the hardest tasks have been met with peace and purpose.

Reflection Question:

Where in your life might God be asking you to pause and listen before acting?

Prayer:

Lord, teach me to pause and hear your voice before I act. Help me to trust your timing and to walk in step with your Spirit. Amen.

Day 23: Wrestling with Doubt

Key Concept:

Trusting God's voice doesn't mean never doubting—it means trusting Him through it.

Scripture:

But Moses said to God, "Who am I that I should go to Pharaoh and bring the Israelites out of Egypt?"

— Exodus 3:11

Reflection:

When I first began to suspect God was calling me into ministry, I obviously had no idea the journey would include a global pandemic or a denominational separation. I had no way to imagine the pain and confusion that would emerge from friends whom I worked with for decades and loved like my kids being called to move on. Yet somehow, I think I knew I needed to be certain God was calling me and was going with me if I was going to be able to make it.

When my soul began to be stirred by what seemed like a calling, I shared it with my father, who was a pastor. He told me my next step was to talk to the District Superintendent to let him know I was exploring a call to ministry. I set up an appointment to talk with the DS and asked him for advice on how I could be sure God was calling me into the ministry. The District Superintendent said, "Glad you are responding to God's call on your life. Go to your local church's Staff Parish Relations Committee and tell them God has called you into the ministry and you are ready to go."

I listened to what he said and replied, "Sir, I am not sure if that is the way to do it."

He said, "Well, that is the way we do it, but how would you suggest doing it?"

I said, "I would like to go to them and say, 'you know me; you have witnessed my walk; you have seen my ministry. Do you think God is calling me into ministry?'"

You see, I didn't want to tell them I was called; I wanted them to tell me I was called! Sure, at that time I felt called, or I wouldn't have even been having that conversation, but somehow, I knew there would come days when I doubted if I had heard correctly. There would be seasons which were so hard and times which were so painful and periods which were so fruitless that I would question if I had ever actually been called. When internal doubts crept in, I wanted to be able to lean on the assurance that those who knew me best and who had witnessed the fruit of my life had declared I was called by God.

Moses doubted his ability to fulfill God's call, and we often do the same. Trusting God's voice doesn't mean we never wrestle with doubts or fears. It means bringing those doubts to Him and allowing His truth to replace our insecurities.

I've had moments when I questioned whether I could handle what God was asking of me. In those times, He reminded me that the call isn't about my ability; it's about His power working through me. Trusting God means believing He is enough, even when we feel we aren't.

Reflection Question:

What doubts are holding you back from fully trusting God's voice? How can you surrender them to Him?

Prayer:

Lord, I bring my doubts to you. Remind me that you are enough and that your strength is made perfect in my weakness. Amen.

Day 24: Learning to Depend on God

Key Concept:

You are not good enough, but that is okay.

Scripture:

And God said, "I will be with you. And this will be the sign to you that it is I who have sent you: When you have brought the people out of Egypt, you will worship God on this mountain."

— Exodus 3:12

Reflection:

If you think you know what God is calling you to do and believe you can do it, then you don't understand what God is calling you to do. His call on your life will always make you aware of your dependence on Him. In fact, the whole point of His calling you is to get you to remain in Him.

I had this old CJ7 jeep. I loved that jeep. It was a great jeep—not dependable but awesome in its own way. I was to speak at an event in Atlanta GA when the Braves were playing at home. I drove up the day before and left early enough to go to the game.

Well, the old CJ7 broke down on the way, but a guy at the filling station got me back on the road and showed me what to do if I broke down again. I was late but made it to the game in the third inning. I had to park a pretty long way from the stadium. As I was preparing to get out of the jeep, I noticed a guy watching me, and it occurred to me that I didn't have any way of locking up my stuff. I didn't have much, but I did have the clothes I needed for my speaking engagement the next day.

As I started to walk off to watch the game, it happened. The spirit convicted me and simultaneously empowered me to love this guy. I went over and introduced myself and invited him to come watch the game with me. He was clearly moved and appreciative but not at all interested in going to see the game. He did, however, keep telling me he was going to stay and watch my jeep because "the robbing crew was coming through."

I went and enjoyed several innings before it started to rain. Not hard enough to end the game but enough to bring me down off my spiritual high to realize I was sitting there while the robbing crew was stealing the only dry clothes I had. I ran back to the jeep and put the key in the ignition to crank it up, but nothing happened. No worries, I knew what to do. I popped the hood and did all the things the mechanic told me to do, but it didn't work. I tried a couple more times and nothing. Then, this man walked up. He didn't look like the robbing crew, but then I don't know what the robbing crew might look like. He said, kind of matter-of-factly, "Got a problem?"

I said, "I think I have it under control."

He correctly replied, "Doesn't look like it." Then. he said, "Let me take a look." He poked his head under the hood and did basically what I had already done, but this time, it worked.

Amazed, I had to ask: "I did the same thing you did, why didn't it work?"

He looked me straight in the face and said, "Because you just aren't good enough."

Wow. There it was. I don't think I have ever been told the truth so bluntly. The sooner we realize we are not good enough, talented enough, or smart enough to do what God is calling us to do, the sooner we will acknowledge our dependance on God, and then God can start doing amazing things in and through us. We don't need talent. We just need God with us.

Reflection Question:

Where and when are you most susceptible to trying to depend on your own ability, connections, or talent?

Prayer:

Lord, today whenever I am tempted to rely on my own ability, remind me to think bigger. Put me in over my head so I will be instantly aware of my dependance on you. Amen.

Day 25: What is Your Name?

Key Concept:

It is always personal to God.

Scripture:

*Moses said to God, "Suppose I go to the Israelites and say to them,
'The God of your fathers has sent me to you,' and they ask me,
'What is his name?' Then what shall I tell them?" God said to Moses, "I AM WHO I AM. This is what you are to say to the Israelites:
'I AM has sent me to you.'"*

— Exodus 3:13–14

Reflection:

The biblical scholars can unpack the depths of meaning to God's answer of "I am who I am," and the historians can explore the insights of Moses' concern that the Israelites might want to know God's name. My mind is drawn to ponder a different point. Is it possible that it was more personal to Moses?

We hear all the time that "someone" wants to know, "people" are wondering, or I'm asking for a "friend." Maybe Moses wants a more personal relationship with God before he takes on this mission. Maybe Moses wants to know the name of the God who is calling him. Maybe it is more personal than professional.

I was running a large youth event, and on this particular night, we had a big Christian band scheduled to come in and do a concert. They required us to empty the auditorium for them to set up and sound check properly before we allowed the mass of students into the building. So, we planned accordingly. As with most youth events, great plans often encounter significant problems. In this case, the problem was the band showed up late and needed more time to set up and sound check after my plan for keeping the students occupied had run its course.

So, then I had a thousand students locked out of the venue, getting more and more worked up to get in. I was having flashbacks of a Who Concert stampede. I was worried someone was going to get hurt. I walked around outside trying to calm the crowd and keep order. It may not have really been a life or death situation, but it felt pretty tense to me.

That was when I heard it. It wasn't loud, but it was familiar, and I recognized it right away. It was little Robbie calling my name, "Jay, Jay, Mr. Jay." I was tempted to ignore it. I mean, I had a situation on my hands; I had important things to do. But, perhaps this was a crisis as well. So, I stopped and turned around. Robbie came running up to me and said, "Mr. Jay the video game took my quarter."

Generally, I tend to speak too quickly. My mom likes to tell me, "Jay boy, everything that pops in your head doesn't have to spill out of your mouth." Fortunately, this time what popped into my mind was the story of the bleeding women. Jesus was being rushed through a large crowd by a father whose child was dying. The crowd undoubtedly was resisting His leaving, and in the middle of it, Jesus stopped and said, "Who touched me?" (Luke 8:45a). The disciples surely pointed out the absurdity of the question because everyone was touching Him, but Jesus noticed this touch was different. It was literally a life-or-death situation with a huge crowd and tons of chaos, and Jesus noticed her. It was personal. It is always personal to Jesus, and I think He wants it to be personal for us as well.

It only took a second. I reached in my pocket and pulled out a quarter for Robbie and gave him a pat on the head as he ran off with his world now having been made right. It was probably the most Christ-like thing I did during the entire event.

Reflection Question:

Who are the people in your life who noticed you, who invested in you?

Prayer:

Lord, thank you for seeing me and sending people into my life to point me to you. You have pursued me all my days, and I will be forever grateful for you and for those through whom you worked to save me. Amen.

Day 26: Passing the Torch

Key Concept:

There is no success without a successor.

Scripture:

Now Joshua son of Nun was filled with the spirit of wisdom because Moses had laid his hands on him. So the Israelites listened to him and did what the LORD had commanded Moses.

— Deuteronomy 34:9

Reflection:

There is no question that Moses was an incredible leader. (Yes, I realize it was God working through him, but you don't see God working like that through everyone.) Sometimes the greatest leadership quality is knowing enough to stay out of God's way. Leading the people out of Egypt is amazing. Leading the people through the wilderness is even more impressive, but what impresses me most is that while the people do eventually enter the promised land, Moses is not the one who leads them in. Joshua does.

Remember that "Vision Quest" to the Moab desert I shared with you way back on Day 2? The reason for that trip was I had a vison to start an outdoor challenge course ministry for developing relationships with yourself, others, and God called Adventure Ministries. Me and some buddies started it, and quickly the vision had become a reality. The "Vision Quest" to the Moab desert was to seek what was next. People told me that is not the way it works, but I pointed out it was how it worked in the Bible, so I was going to listen to God in the wilderness.

It was certainly quite an adventure, and upon returning, people wanted to know if I had heard what was next for Adventure Ministries. The odd thing was I hadn't heard anything, but I somehow knew what needed to happen had happened. I didn't know what was next for Adventure Ministries, or for me for that matter, but I knew it was handled.

I can still remember walking around the ropes course holding my new baby, Cole, thinking Adventure Ministries would be the greatest thing I ever did. I went on to do many more things after starting Adventure Ministries, but I don't think I was ever more fulfilled or satisfied than the times I was working with groups out on the course. Eventually, I left Epworth and stopped running Adventure Ministries to go run another ministry. Epworth sold Adventure Ministries to another group, which took it in a slightly different direction. Meanwhile, life moved on for me and my family. Cole and Summer grew up and went off to college. Summer graduated and became a flight attendant for Delta and traveled all over the world. Cole moved out west to do some crazy wilderness stuff. Kim and I were very proud of them both.

Cole's job was seasonal, and when it ended, he called to say he was coming home for a season. About that time, I got another call from Joel Willis, who was the head of Epworth by the Sea. Apparently, the ropes course had been sold a couple of times, and the current owner was moving on, and Joel wanted to know if I would be interested in taking over again and restarting Adventure Ministries. Talk about perfect timing. I checked with Cole, and he was all about it. So now, Cole runs Adventure Ministries, and it is twice as great as it ever was when I was running it. He does an amazing job, and if you are ever in need of some incredible faith and team building, you should certainly bring your group down to the Georgia Coast and check out Adventure Ministries.

...Did I mention Cole was conceived in Moab on the "Vision Quest?"

Reflection Question:

Who is your Joshua, your Timothy, your Tabitha, your Donna?

Prayer:

Lord, help me see who you are sending me to walk beside today and help me be a good friend to them. Amen.

Day 27: Practical Application: Finding Your Five Friends

Key Concept:

Identify the people God wants you to befriend.

Action Step:

1. Look for five people to befriend:
   a. **Pay attention to those around you.** Is there an acquaintance who you're bumping into more often?
   b. **Notice who is paying attention to you.** They look you in the eye and listen when you talk.
   c. **Listen to their life.** Does what they say or do suggest they might be seeking something?
   d. **Hang out with them.** Spend time with them. Invite them to coffee or lunch.
2. **Ask God to show you five people** in your life that He wants you to befriend.

Refection Questions:

Is your intimacy with God producing within you a passion for the lost? If not, why do you think that is?

Prayer:

Lord, help me to experience true intimacy with you that naturally produces a passion within me for those who don't know you. Lord, open my eyes to the people you have placed in my life for me to love. Amen.

Day 28: Rest, Recap, & Reflect

Key Concept:

Listening to God will always lead to sharing what He says.

Recap:

This week we looked at how God's "sending" is really more of an invitation to come with Him. Our relationship with God is far more essential than our responsibilities. It is personal to God, and He wants us to learn to depend on Him.

Seek God! Share what He shows you. Serve where He sends you.

There is a chance He will "send" you to a place, but it is far more likely He is going to invite you to go with Him to build a relationship with someone.

Reflection Questions:

What have you learned about listening to God over these past four weeks?

What do you think God might be trying to say to you?

How do you think He might want you to respond?

Prayer:

Lord, do with me today whatever you must so that in the future you may do with me whatever you wish. Amen.

SCAN HERE to learn more about
Invite Ministries—created to invite people to a deeper
faith and living relationship with Jesus Christ